W9-BRH-212

WORKBOOK: HOMEWORK AND CHARACTER BOOK
作業和寫字簿
to Accompany

Chinese Link

中　文　天　地
Zhōng　　Wén　　Tiān　　Dì

Elementary Chinese

Traditional Character Version

吳素美　　　　于月明　　　　張燕輝　　　　田維忠
Sue-mei Wu　　Yueming Yu　　Yanhui Zhang　　Weizhong Tian

Carnegie Mellon University

PEARSON
Prentice Hall

woRLd Languages

Upper Saddle River, New Jersey 07458

Acquisitions Editor: Rachel McCoy
Publishing Coordinator: Claudia Fernandes
Executive Director of Market Development: Kristine Suárez
Director of Editorial Development: Julia Caballero
Production Supervision: Nancy Stevenson
Project Manager: Margaret Chan, Graphicraft
Assistant Director of Production: Mary Rottino
Supplements Editor: Meriel Martínez Moctezuma
Media Editor: Samantha Alducin
Media Production Manager: Roberto Fernandez
Prepress and Manufacturing Buyer: Christina Helder
Prepress and Manufacturing Assistant Manager: Mary Ann Gloriande
Cover Art Director: Jayne Conte
Marketing Assistant: William J. Bliss
Publisher: Phil Miller
Cover image: Jerry Darvin

This book was set in 12/15 Sabon by Graphicraft Ltd., Hong Kong, and was printed and bound by BRR. The cover was printed by BRR.

© 2007 by Pearson Education, Inc.
Upper Saddle River, NJ 07458

Printed in the United States of America
10 9 8 7 6 5 4 3 2 1

ISBN 0-13-242976-4

Pearson Education Ltd., *London*
Pearson Education Australia Pty, Limited, *Sydney*
Pearson Education Singapore Pte. Ltd.
Pearson Education North Asia Ltd., *Hong Kong*
Pearson Education Canada, Ltd., *Toronto*
Pearson Educación de México, S.A. de C.V.
Pearson Education – Japan, *Tokyo*
Pearson Education Malaysia Pte. Ltd.
Pearson Education, *Upper Saddle River,* New Jersey

目錄 CONTENTS

Character Book Indices

拼音作業一　Pinyin Homework I

Simple finals: a o e i u ü　　　*Labial initials: b p m f*　　　*Alveolar initials: d t n l*

1-1 Listen and circle the right final:

1. lǖ　lǘ　lǚ　lǜ　　　5. dē　dé　dě　dè

2. fū　fú　fǔ　fù　　　6. mō　mó　mǒ　mò

3. pī　pí　pǐ　pì　　　7. tī　tí　tǐ　tì

4. nā　ná　nǎ　nà　　　8. bā　bá　bǎ　bà

1-2 Listen and circle the right initial:

1. mù　nù　　　4. lǔ　nǔ　　　7. lǚ　nǚ　　　10. nǐ　lǐ

2. pā　tā　　　5. pà　bà　　　8. bè　tè　　　11. tā　lā

3. mó　fó　　　6. tè　lè　　　9. dí　tí　　　12. pū　mū

1-3 Listen and fill in the blanks with the right sound:

1. _____　　6. _____　　11. _____　　16. _____

2. _____　　7. _____　　12. _____　　17. _____

3. _____　　8. _____　　13. _____　　18. _____

4. _____　　9. _____　　14. _____　　19. _____

5. _____　　10. _____　　15. _____　　20. _____

Velar initials: g k h   *Palatal initials: j q x*
Dental sibilant initials: z c s *Retroflex initials: zh ch sh r*

2-1 Listen and circle the right initial:

1. qì xì	6. zhè zè	11. cǐ sǐ	16. rè chè
2. xī sī	7. jī qī	12. shú chú	17. cā zā
3. shī sī	8. rì shì	13. hù rù	18. gé hé
4. jǐ xǐ	9. zhà chà	14. lè gè	19. cū sū
5. cè chè	10. zǔ sǔ	15. xì shì	20. gē kē

2-2 Listen and fill in the blank with the right initial:

1. ____ē	11. ____à	21. ____é
2. ____ī	12. ____ú	22. ____á
3. ____è	13. ____ǐ	23. ____ě
4. ____ī	14. ____è	24. ____ì
5. ____ā	15. ____ì	25. ____ū
6. ____í	16. ____è	26. ____ǎ
7. ____ù	17. ____ù	27. ____ì
8. ____ì	18. ____è	28. ____ǔ
9. ____ū	19. ____ǐ	29. ____é
10. ____ē	20. ____ì	30. ____ù

拼音作業三 Pinyin Homework III

Compound finals: ai ei ao ou   ia iao ie iu   ua uo uai ui   üe

3-1 Listen and mark the right tones:

1. lao	6. hou	11. kuo	16. nuo
2. cui	7. hua	12. pei	17. hui
3. zhua	8. ai	13. shuo	18. biao
4. liu	9. lüe	14. bie	19. tou
5. ren	10. shuai	15. zhou	20. mao

3-2 Listen and circle the right sounds:

1. chóu zhóu	6. cáo cái	11. jiǎo xiǎo	16. bǎo biǎo
2. chāo qiāo	7. lái léi	12. bié béi	17. shāo xiāo
3. dōu duō	8. lín liú	13. lüè nüè	18. luó lóu
4. jué xué	9. dāo dōu	14. xuē xiū	19. guò gòu
5. huó hóu	10. diū duī	15. rào ròu	20. jiā jiē

3-3 Listen and fill in the blanks with the right finals:

1. b_____	8. l_____	15. zh_____
2. p_____	9. g_____	16. ch_____
3. m_____	10. k_____	17. sh_____
4. f _____	11. h_____	18. r_____
5. d_____	12. j_____	19. z_____
6. t_____	13. q_____	20. c_____
7. n_____	14. x_____	21. s_____

Nasal finals:　*an en*　　　*ian in*　　　*uan un*
　　　　　　　ang eng ong　*iang ing iong*　*uang*

4-1　Listen and mark the right tones:

1. jiong	6. lun	11. hen	16. nuan
2. xian	7. rong	12. qiang	17. zhuang
3. hun	8. fen	13. heng	18. zhun
4. an	9. cang	14. liang	19. sun
5. qin	10. mian	15. ling	20. ding

4-2　Listen and circle the right sounds:

1. juān　jūn	6. lín　líng	11. xióng　qióng	16. cóng　chóng
2. zhèn　shèn	7. tūn　tuān	12. zhàn　zhèn	17. zhāng　jiāng
3. qiáng　qióng	8. rēng　zhēng	13. háng　huáng	18. xūn　sūn
4. xiàng　xuàn	9. kàn　kèn	14. huán　huáng	19. gèn　gèng
5. rǎn　zhǎn	10. qǐng　xǐng	15. jūn　qūn	20. nián　lián

4-3　Listen and fill in the blanks with the right finals:

1. b_____	8. l_____	15. zh_____
2. p_____	9. g_____	16. ch_____
3. m_____	10. k_____	17. sh_____
4. f_____	11. h_____	18. r_____
5. d_____	12. j_____	19. z_____
6. t_____	13. q_____	20. c_____
7. n_____	14. x_____	21. s_____

拼音作業五　Pinyin Homework V

Special Pinyin and tonal rules

5-1 Listen and fill in the blanks with the right Pinyin:

1. _____   6. _____   11. _____   16. _____

2. _____   7. _____   12. _____   17. _____

3. _____   8. _____   13. _____   18. _____

4. _____   9. _____   14. _____   19. _____

5. _____   10. _____   15. _____   20. _____

5-2 Mark the tones of "yi" (一) and "bu" (不) in accordance with the "yi-bu" tonal rules:

1. ___wǔ___shí
   一五一十

2. ___xīn___yì
   一心一意

3. ___zhāo___xī
   一朝一夕

4. ___chàng___hè
   一唱一和

5. ___mó___yàng
   一模一樣

6. ___wén___wèn
   不聞不問

7. ___míng___bái
   不明不白

8. ___zhé___kòu
   不折不扣

9. ___sān___sì
   不三不四

10. ___bēi___kàng
    不卑不亢

11. ____ sī___gǒu
    一絲不苟

12. ____ chéng___biàn
    一成不變

13. ___wén___zhí
    一文不值

14. ___qiào___tōng
    一竅不通

15. ___chén___rǎn
    一塵不染

Comprehensive Pinyin Review

6-1 Listen and circle the right sounds:

1. dàng	dèng	6. lǔ	liǔ	11. yǔ	yǒu	16. zhàn	jiàn
2. lǔ	nǔ	7. bīn	bīng	12. lián	liáng	17. yuǎn	yǎn
3. wō	ōu	8. niè	lèi	13. xiōng	jiōng	18. jiǎo	xiǎo
4. jié	zéi	9. dōu	tōu	14. kǒu	gǒu	19. xiù	shòu
5. jūn	zhēn	10. zuō	cuō	15. xià	xiào	20. cāi	sāi

6-2 Listen to the following classroom expressions. Then write them in Pinyin:

1. _____

2. _____

3. _____

4. _____

5. _____

6. _____

7. _____

8. _____

9. _____

10. _____

Lesson 1   Hello!

I. Listening Exercises

A. Listen and write out the initials for each of the following words:

1. ____ì   2. ____a   3. ____ué____eng

4. ____ǎo____ī   5. ____e   6. ____ú

B. Listen and fill in the blanks with appropriate finals:

1. W____   sh____   x____sh____.

2. T____   b____sh ____   l____sh____ , t____   sh____   x____sh____.

3. N____   y____   b____sh____   x____sh____   m____?

C. Listen to the dialogue and then mark each statement below as True (✓) or False (✗):

MARY: 你好!

JOHN: 你好!

MARY: 我是學生，你也是學生嗎?

JOHN: 不。我是老師。

☐ 1. Mary 是學生。   ☐ 3. Mary 不是學生。

☐ 2. John 也是學生。   ☐ 4. John 是老師。

D. Listen to the dialogue again and write it out in Pinyin:

_____

_____

_____

_____

II. Character Exercises

A. Write out the characters for the following Pinyin:

1. tā _____   2. wǒ _____   3. shì _____   4. shī _____

5. nǐ _____   6. xué _____   7. ne _____   8. lǎo _____

9. yě _____   10. sheng _____   11. bú _____   12. hǎo _____

B. Write out the Chinese characters for each of the following words and then show its stroke order:

English	Character	Stroke order
you		
to be		
student		

C. Write the Chinese characters for the following English words:

1. he _____   2. fine _____   3. teacher _____

4. I _____   5. also _____   6. student _____

7. not _____   8. you _____

III. Grammar Exercises

A. Fill in the blanks in the following dialogue with " 嗎 " or " 呢 ":

A: 你好！

B: 你好！

A: 我是學生，你也是學生 _____?

B: 我也是學生。

A: 他 _____? 他也是學生 _____?

B: 不，他是老師。

B. Complete the following sentences with the help of the clues:

1. 你 _____ 。(a greeting)

2. 我 _____ 。(to be a student)

3. 你 _____ 學生嗎? (to be also)

4. 他也 _____ 老師 。(to be not)

5. 你 _____? (question — how about) 你 _____ 老師嗎? (to be not, either)

C. Insert the words in parentheses at the appropriate place(s) in each sentence. Write the sentences in the space provided.

1. 他學生 。(是)

   _____

2. 我是學生，你是學生? (也、嗎)

   _____

3. 他是老師，他學生。(不、是)

   _____

IV. Comprehensive Exercises

A. Rearrange the following boxes to form a dialogue. Write the number before each sentence to show the correct order:

Correct order

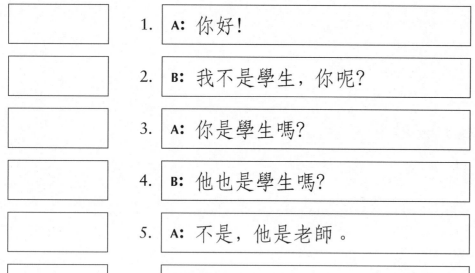

1. | A: 你好!

2. | B: 我不是學生，你呢?

3. | A: 你是學生嗎?

4. | B: 他也是學生嗎?

5. | A: 不是，他是老師。

6. | B: 你好!

7. | A: 我是學生。

B. Complete the dialogue with the help of the clues:

A: 你好!

B: _____!

A: 我是學生，_____?

B: 我不是學生，_____ 。

A: 他 _____ 老師嗎?

B: 是，_____ 。

Lesson 2   What's Your Surname?

I. Listening Exercises

A. Listen and circle the correct Pinyin in each pair:

1. qǐngwèn
   Yīngwén

2. tóngxué
   tóngshì

3. nǐ jiào shénme
   nǐ xiào shénme

4. míngcí
   míngzi

5. shuí cuò
   shéi shuō

B. Listen to the dialogues and circle the correct answer:

1. The person's family name is

   a. Hú.

   b. Lú.

   c. Wú.

2. a. Wenying is a teacher.

   b. Xiaomei's classmate is a teacher.

   c. Dazhong Li is Wenying's classmate.

3. a. Yu Ying's teacher is Xuewen Wu.

   b. Yu Ying is a teacher.

   c. Yu Ying is the man's name.

II. Character Exercises

A. Write out the radicals in the following groups of characters:

☐	好　她　姓
☐	嗎　叫　呢
☐	請　誰

B. Write the simplified form of the following characters:

學
□

誰
□

師
□

嗎
□

問
□

C. Translate the following Pinyin sentences into Chinese:

1. Qǐngwèn, nín shì Lǐ lǎoshī ma?

_____

2. Nǐde tóngxué jiào shénme míngzi?

_____

III. Grammar Exercises

A. Please use the following clues to make as many sentences as you can. You need to include positive statements, negative statements, and questions. You may use each word as many times as you need:

李，學文，叫，您，姓，名字，中文，是，請問，我
吳，老師，她，于，的，小美，同學，不，什麼，嗎

_____

_____

_____

_____

_____

B. Ask a question on the underlined part in the following sentences (use the underlined part as the answer to your question):

1. 我姓<u>吳</u>。_____?

2. <u>她</u>叫李小英。_____?

3. 他是<u>我的同學</u>。_____?

4. 我的中文名字是<u>于文漢</u>。_____?

C. Translate the following phrases into Chinese:

1. My teacher's name   _____

2. His classmates   _____

3. Wenzhong Li's student   _____

4. Your Chinese name   _____

5. Her student's Chinese name _____

IV. Comprehensive Exercises

A. Complete the following dialogue:

A: 你好! 請問, _____?

B: 我 _____ 李, _____ 學文。你呢?

A: _____ 叫吳小英。我 _____ 學生。

B: 她是 _____? 她 _____ 學生嗎?

A: 不, 她是 _____ 。

B: 她是 _____ 中文老師嗎?

A: 不, _____ 我的英文老師。

B. You introduced yourself to all the students in the Chinese class today. Write down what you said in class about yourself. You may add whatever information you want to help others know you better (approximately 50 characters).

_____

_____

_____

_____

_____

_____

Lesson 3   Which Country Are You From?

I. Listening Exercises

A. Listen and circle the six words you hear:

1. Fǎguó	2. shòumìng	3. Zhōngwén	4. Měilìjiān
5. bāgè	6. shuōmíng	7. měiyìjiā	8. chōngwén
9. Yīngwén	10. nǎr		

B. Listen and add the correct tone mark(s) to the following Pinyin:

1. cong	2. Hanyu	3. xuexi	4. nar	5. mingtian
6. guojia	7. yuyan	8. xingming	9. jiaoshou	10. shuohua

C. Listen to the dialogue and write it out in Pinyin, paying special attention to the tones:

_____

_____

_____

_____

II. Character Exercises

A. Write out each stroke of the following characters in the appropriate order:

國 _____

美 _____

說 _____

哪 _____

B. Write out as many characters as you can that use the radicals below:

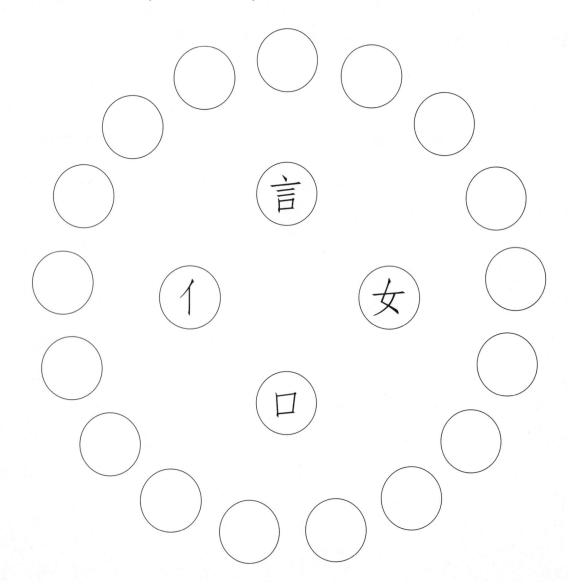

III. Grammar Exercises

A. Complete the following sentences with the help of the clues:

1. 你是 _____ 人？

   我是 _____ 。　　　　(英國)

2. 我是 _____人。　　　(中國)

   我說 _____ 。

3. 他是 _____ 。

   他教 _____ 。　　　　(英文)

   Note: 教 [jiāo]: to teach

4. 我會 _____ 。　　　　(英)

   我也會 _____ 。　　　(法)

B. Complete the following sentences:

1. 小文是 _____ ，他 _____ 中文。

2. 李小美 _____ 法國人，她 ____ 說英文，她說 _____ 。

3. 她 ____ 美國人，她說 _____ ，她 ____ 說 _____ 日文。

   Note: 日文 [Rìwén]: Japanese language

IV. Comprehensive Exercises

Someone asks you about your friend who is also in your class. Use the list you compiled in class as a reference to introduce him/her to others. Write as much as you can about your friend (approximately 60 characters).

_____

_____

_____

_____

_____

_____

Lesson 4   What Do You Study?

I. Listening Exercises

A. Listen to the dialogues and fill in the blanks with Pinyin:

1. Zhè shì shénme?

   Zhè shì _____.

   Gōngchéng _____?

   _____.

2. _____ shéi?

   Nà shì _____.

   Tā _____ ma?

   Tā _____.

3. Nǐ xué _____?

   Wǒ xué _____.

   Zhōngwén _____?

   Bú _____, kěshì _____.

II. Character Exercises

A. Write out the Chinese character for each of the following words and then show its stroke order:

English	Character	Stroke order
this		
difficult		
engineering		
homework		

B. Give the radical for the following characters and see whether you can provide more examples of characters with the same radical:

Radical　　　Examples

1. 課 ☐ _____

2. 你 ☐ _____

3. 嗎 ☐ _____

III. Grammar Exercises

A. Ask as many questions as you can on the following sentences:

Example:	這是中文書。 一 這是什麼? 一 這是什麼書?

1. 這是文中的一本工程書。

   _____

   _____

   _____

2. 工程課的功課很多。

   _____

   _____

   _____

3. 英國文學不太難。

   _____

   _____

   _____

4. 中文功課很多,也很難。

   _____

   _____

IV. Comprehensive Exercises

A. Translate the following sentences into Chinese:

1. Who is he? He is my Chinese literature professor.

   _____

2. What is that? That is an engineering book. That is a book in English.

   _____

3. What do you study? I study French literature. French literature is not very difficult, but there is a lot of homework.

   _____

B. You are going to attend a meeting called by your department. The meeting is to collect your comments on your study and life on campus. The department needs to have some basic information about you before the meeting. Write out a paragraph to introduce yourself (approximately 70 characters).

_____

_____

_____

_____

_____

_____

_____

Lesson 5   This Is My Friend

I. Listening Exercises

A. Listen to the dialogue and mark each of the following sentences with a "✓" if it is correct, an "✗" if it is wrong:

☐ 1. Xiǎohóng de shìyǒu jiào Měiwén.

☐ 2. Měiwén hé Fāng Míng dōu shì Zhōngguórén.

☐ 3. Fāng Míng jièshào tāde péngyou Xiǎohóng.

☐ 4. Měiwén cháng gēn Xiǎohóng shuō Zhōngwén.

☐ 5. Xiǎohóng yǒu liǎngge Měiguó shìyǒu.

B. Listen to the dialogue and fill in the blanks with correct words or expressions:

吳小英：大文，我來＿＿＿＿ 一下。＿＿＿＿ 我室友王小紅。

李大文：＿＿＿＿ 李大文。你好!

王小紅：你好! 你是學生＿＿＿＿?

李大文：是。我＿＿＿ 工程。你＿＿＿?

王小紅：我學＿＿＿＿ 。我＿＿＿ 小英＿＿＿ 同學。我們＿＿ 學
＿＿＿＿ 文學。

II. Character Exercises

A. Pick from this lesson as many characters as you can that start with a horizontal stroke
(⁻):

1. _____   2. _____   3. _____   4. _____   5. _____   6. _____

7. _____

With a vertical stroke (|):

1. _____   2. _____

With a left-slanted stroke (ノ):

1. _____   2. _____   3. _____   4. _____   5. _____   6. _____

7. _____

B. Turn the following Pinyin into characters:

1. liǎngge péngyou _____

2. jǐge shìyǒu _____

3. jièshào yíxià _____

4. cháng shuō Zhōngwén _____

III. Grammar Exercises

A. Fill in the blanks in the following paragraph. Read it carefully and then ask as many questions on the paragraph as you can:

方美文＿＿＿＿ 中文班的學生。她＿＿＿＿ 一個室友，＿＿＿＿ 王文英。

王文英＿＿＿＿ 中國人。她＿＿＿＿ 一個男朋友，＿＿＿＿ 李中。

李中是美國＿＿＿＿，他＿＿＿＿ 學中文。他常＿＿＿＿ 文英說中文。

他們＿＿＿＿ 是好朋友。

Note: 班 [bān]: class

_____

_____

_____

_____

_____

_____

_____

IV. Comprehensive Exercises

You share an apartment with your classmates, Wáng Fāng and Lǐ Yīng. You have invited your friend Wú Xiǎowén to come for a party at your apartment. Introduce them and then have a conversation. Write out the conversation using as much from the lesson as you can.

_____

_____

_____

_____

_____

_____

_____

Lesson 6   My Family

I. Listening Exercises

A. Listen, then read the following sentences. Mark "✓" if the statement is correct, and "✗" if it is wrong:

☐ 1. Jiāmíng hé Yǒupéng dōushì cóng Táiwān lái de.

☐ 2. Yǒupéng de bàba bù hěn máng.

☐ 3. Jiāmíng méiyǒu nán péngyou, tā jiějie yǒu.

☐ 4. Yǒupéng de jiā búzài Niǔyuē, zài Bōshìdùn.

☐ 5. Jiāmíng de mèimei méiyǒu māo, yǒu liǎngzhī gǒu.

B. Listen to the paragraph and answer the questions in Pinyin:

1. _____

2. _____

3. _____

4. _____

5. _____

II. Character Exercises

A. Circle the radicals in the following characters:

1. 輛   2. 爸   3. 姐   4. 程

5. 作   6. 狗   7. 沒   8. 課

B. Write the following sentences in characters:

1. Wǒ jiā yǒu sìge rén. _____

2. Jiějie yǒu yíge nán péngyou. _____

3. Bàba, māma dōu shì zài Měiguó gōngzuò de. _____

4. Wǒ yǒu liǎngzhī gǒu. _____

5. Wǒ hěn ài wǒde jiā. _____

III. Grammar Exercises

A. Fill in the blank of each phrase with a proper measure word (classifier):

1. 一 _____ 車   2. 一 _____ 狗

3. 兩 _____ 學生   4. 三 _____ 書

B. Fill in the blanks in the following paragraph and then ask questions on the highlighted parts:

小美的家 _____。他家有 _____人：爸爸、媽媽、姐姐和她。爸爸、媽媽都在紐約 _____。爸爸有兩 _____車， _____是日本車。姐姐 _____有一輛車，是德國車。姐姐的男朋友 _____家文，他是 _____來的。

Note: 波士頓 [Bōshìdùn]: Boston

_____

_____

_____

_____

IV. Comprehensive Exercises

A. Translate the following sentences into Chinese:

1. Both Xiaoying and her boyfriend are from China.

   _____

2. My roommate has an American car.

   _____

3. There are four people in my family. We all love our family.

   _____

B. You received an email from 李書文, a student in China who is looking for a pen pal. You have been looking for a Chinese pen pal for a while. Now you want to take this opportunity to make friends with him. Write an introduction about yourself and then ask him some questions to get to know him better.

Note: 筆友 [bǐyǒu]: pen pal

_____

_____

_____

_____

Lesson 7   Where Do You Live?

I. Listening Exercises

A. Listen to the dialogue and circle the right answer:

1. 小美住在哪兒?

   a. 住在宿舍。

   b. 住在校外。

   c. 住在朋友家。

   d. 住在公寓。

2. 小美的房間號碼是多少?

   a. 二三五

   b. 五二三

   c. 九二三

   d. 二八五

3. 小美的手機號碼是多少?

   a. 三三二 二六八七四六九

   b. 七七二 二二八四七六九

   c. 五三三 六八六二四九七

   d. 八八二 九二八四六七三

4. 小美有幾個室友?

   a. 二個

   b. 兩個

   c. 三個

   d. 一個

B. Listen to the dialogue and fill in the blanks with the correct Pinyin:

常小西: 書文,你住在那個_____ 嗎?

程書文: 不,我住在_____,房間號碼是_____。

常小西: 你的_____ 有_____ 嗎?

程書文: 沒有_____,可是我有_____。

常小西: 號碼是_____?

程書文: 號碼是_____。

Note: 公寓 [gōngyù]: apartment

II. Character Exercises

A. Comprehensive character exercises:

Process 1: Write down the radical.

Process 2: Count strokes of the character.

Process 3: Write down the correct Pinyin for the character.

Process 4: Make as many words or phrases using the character as you can.

Example: 房 → 戶 → 8 → fáng → 房間

	Radical	No. of strokes	Pinyin	Word
1. 間				
2. 號				
3. 校				
4. 機				

B. Write down the simplified form of the framed characters.

1. 哪 兒 _____   2. 號 碼 _____

3. 房 間 _____   4. 電 話 _____

5. 手 機 _____

III. Grammar Exercises

A. 大王 and 小李 are in the same Chinese class. They often work together in class. Now the professor asks them to find out each other's contact information for future use. Complete the conversation by filling in the blanks with what you have learned in this lesson:

大王：小李，你 ____ 在宿舍嗎？

小李：對了，我 ____ 在學校的 _____ 。你 ____ 住在學校的宿舍嗎？

大王：不，我住在校外，在 _____
　　　　　　　　　　　　　　(Number 89764 Fifth Ave.)

小李：你的房間 _____ 嗎？

大王：很大， ____ 很好 。你住在 _____ ？

小李：二〇八號 。我的房間 ____ 不小 。你的電話號碼 _____ ？

大王： _____ (103-952-8467)

小李：我的電話號碼 _____ 六四八二五三一 。

Note: 對了 [duìle]: yes, correct; by the way

Hint: Fifth Ave.: 第五大街 [dì wǔ dàjiē]

B. Translate the following sentences into Chinese:

1. Where do you live?

   _____

2. Do you live on campus?

   _____

3. My brother's dorm is not big.

   _____

4. Your cellular phone number is (142)268-5738, isn't it?

   _____

IV. Comprehensive Exercises

Write a note:

Your close friend is going to visit you over the weekend. Please write a short note providing necessary information such as your address, phone number, and roommates' names, etc.

_____

_____

_____

_____

_____

_____

Lesson 8   Do You Know Him?

I. Listening Exercises

A. Listen to the sentences. Translate the question into English and write the answer in Pinyin:

> Example:
>
> Dialogue on the tape:
>
> 韓文英: 你認識的中國同學多不多?
> 謝國友: 很多。
>
> *Your answers:*
>
> Translated question: *Do you know a lot of Chinese students?*
> Pinyin answer: *Hěnduō.*

1. Translated question: _____

   Pinyin answer: _____

2. Translated question: _____

   Pinyin answer: _____

3. Translated question: _____

   Pinyin answer: _____

4. Translated question: _____

   Pinyin answer: _____

5. Translated question: _____

   Pinyin answer: _____

B. Listen to the dialogue and circle the correct answer:

1. 德朋是從哪兒來的?
   a. 中國　　　　b. 韓國　　　　c. 紐約　　　　d. 日本

2. 文中、德朋和王紅今天想去吃什麼菜?
   a. 中國菜　　　b. 韓國菜　　　c. 泰國菜　　　d. 日本菜

3. 他們下次想去吃什麼菜?
   a. 中國菜　　　b. 韓國菜　　　c. 泰國菜　　　d. 日本菜

II. Character Exercises

A. Write down the simplified forms of the following characters, and then mark their radicals:

Example: 麼 ［么］［广］

	Simplified form	Radical		Simplified form	Radical		Simplified form	Radical
1. 認			2. 識			3. 課		
4. 後			5. 飯			6. 樣		

B. Write the following sentences in characters:

1. Nǐ yǒu shénme shèr ma?

   _____

2. Nǐ xiǎng bù xiǎng huí jiā?

   _____

3. Wǒmen yìqǐ qù Zhōngguó, hǎo bù hǎo?

   _____

4. Xiàkè yǐhòu wǒ xiǎng qù péngyou jiā.

   _____

5. Wǒ bú rènshi nà ge gōngchéngshī.

   _____

III. Grammar Exercises

A. Change the following sentences into interrogative forms by adding the words given in the brackets at the appropriate places:

1. 吳小美是學工程的。　(是嗎)

   _____

2. 她今天想回家。　(A 不 A)

   _____

3. 張友朋認識我姐姐。　(對不對)

   _____

4. 他的兩個室友都是美國人。　(嗎)

   _____

5. 我們下次一起去紐約。　(怎麼樣)

   _____

6. 下課以後我去吃飯。　(A 不 A)

   _____

B. Translate the following sentences into Chinese:

1. Where are you going?

   _____

2. I have a plan for after class.

   _____

3. Do you want to have dinner with us tonight?

   _____

4. My friend doesn't know our English teacher.

   _____

IV. Comprehensive Exercises

Write a dialogue:

You are going to invite your Chinese friend, 文英, to watch an American movie after class. Please write down the short dialogue between you and 文英. Please use more "A 不 A" questions and tag questions in the dialogue.

_____

_____

_____

_____

_____

_____

_____

Lesson 9　He Is Making a Phone Call

I.　Listening Exercises

A. Listen to the dialogue and circle the right answer:

1. 丁明在哪兒?
   a. 在紐約
   b. 在他的房間
   c. 在朋友家
   d. 在宿舍

2. 丁明在做什麼?
   a. 在看電視
   b. 在練習中文
   c. 在上課
   d. 在吃日本菜

3. 今天晚上丁明想做什麼?
   a. 想看電影
   b. 想去朋友家
   c. 想看小說
   d. 想上網

4. 和丁明打電話的是誰?
   a. 愛文
   b. 小美
   c. 丁明的妹妹
   d. 王紅

B. Listen to the telephone messages and mark the correct statements with "✓" and the incorrect ones with "✗":

☐ 1. 電話是小西的同學打來的。

☐ 2. 打電話的人今天晚上想和小西一起去看電影。

☐ 3. 他的電話號碼是(一四二)三六六七八九二。

Note: 電影 [diànyǐng]: movie

II. Pinyin and Character Exercises

A. Circle the correct Pinyin to match the words:

1.	正在	zèngzài	zhèngzài	zèngzhài
2.	房間	hángjiān	féngjiàn	fángjiān
3.	電視	diànsì	diànshì	diánshì
4.	上網	shángwǎng	shàngwǎng	shánghuǎng
5.	時候	shíhou	shéhou	chíhou
6.	今天	zīntiān	jíntian	jīntiān
7.	晚上	wǎngsàng	wánchàng	wǎnshàng
8.	留言	lúyán	niúyán	liúyán
9.	再見	zàijiàn	zhàijiàn	zhuáizhuàn
10.	知道	jīdào	jídòu	zhīdào

B. Comprehensive character exercises:

Process 1: Write down the radical.

Process 2: Count strokes of the character.

Process 3: Write down the correct Pinyin for the character.

Process 4: Make as many words or phrases using the character as you can.

Example: 話 → 言 → 13 → huà → 電話

	Radical	No. of strokes	Pinyin	Word
1. 今				
2. 看				
3. 電				
4. 忙				

C. Write down the simplified form of the framed characters:

1. 打 電 話 _____   2. 看 電 視 _____

3. 上 網 _____   4. 看 書 _____

5. 對 不 起 _____   6. 時 候 _____

7. 謝謝 _____   8. 給 _____

III. Grammar Exercises

A. Complete the sentences with "正在 ......" and the phrases given:

1. **A:** 請問小文在嗎?

   B: 在,他_____。(看電視)

2. **A:** 丁老師呢?

   B: 她 _____。(休息)

3. **A:** 姐姐呢?

   B: 她 _____。(和男朋友打電話)

4. **A:** 王紅和小美都在學中文嗎?

   B: 王紅沒有在學中文。她 _____。(學法文)

B. Translate the following sentences into Chinese:

1. Do you want to leave a message?

   _____

2. Please ask him to call me when he is back.

   _____

3. May I ask who is speaking, please?

   _____

4. He is not watching TV. He is on the Internet.

   _____

5. Hold on, please.

   _____

IV. Comprehensive Exercises

Leave a message:

You want to go to 小文's dorm to ask him some questions on mathematics this evening, but 小文 is not available when you visit him. Compose a message to leave on his answering machine, telling him about your plan and asking him to call you back when he returns.

   _____

   _____

   _____

   _____

   _____

Lesson 10　I Get Up at 7:30 Every Day

I. Listening Exercises

A. Listen to 小美's daily schedule of her summer Chinese course in Shanghai, and then mark the correct statements with "✓" and the incorrect ones with "✗":

☐ 1. 小美每天早上八點起床。

☐ 2. 然後九點去學校上課。

☐ 3. 下課以後，小美去圖書館看書。

☐ 4. 下午小美上中文課。

☐ 5. 中文課以後，小美去打球。

B. Listen to 友朋 talk about his daily schedule and write out the time of each activity in Chinese:

1. 起床　　　　2. 睡覺　　　　3. 上課　　　　4. 吃晚飯

_____　_____　_____　_____

5. 去圖書館　　6. 打球　　　　7. 學中文　　　8. 上網

_____　_____　_____　_____

II. Pinyin and Character Exercises

Write out the Pinyin and characters for the following English words or phrases:

	Pinyin	character		Pinyin	character
1. university	_____	_____	2. semester	_____	_____
3. everyday	_____	_____	4. life	_____	_____
5. email	_____	_____	6. library	_____	_____
7. then	_____	_____	8. like	_____	_____
9. write letter	_____	_____	10. play ball	_____	_____
11. get up	_____	_____	12. go to bed	_____	_____

III. Grammar Exercises

A. The following time and activities show what 文英 does every day. Write a paragraph about her daily activities:

10:30 A.M. (use "才")	get up
11:30 A.M. every day	take courses
after class	play ball
4:00 P.M.	study in the library
8:30 P.M.	write emails
12:15 A.M.	sleep

_____

_____

_____

_____

_____

B. Translate the following sentences into Chinese:

1. He went to have Japanese food at 12:30. After that, he went to the library.

   _____

2. I wrote a letter to my elder sister after getting up.

   _____

3. He plays ball at 9:00 P.M. every day.

   _____

4. I like my university life.

   _____

IV. Comprehensive Exercises

Short essay:

Write a letter describing your university life to your parents.

_____

_____

_____

_____

_____

_____

_____

Lesson 11　Do You Want Black Tea or Green Tea?

I. Listening Exercises

A. Listen to the dialogue and mark the correct statements with "✓" and the incorrect ones with "✗":

☐ 1. 小美和于英正在法國飯館吃飯。

☐ 2. 小美正在喝湯。

☐ 3. 飯館的牛肉很好吃。

☐ 4. 于英不喜歡喝可樂。

B. Listen to the telephone conversation between 方小文 and a waitress in a Chinese restaurant. Check the items and circle the numbers 方小文 has ordered for pick-up.

Note: 拿 [ná]: pick up

方小文點的菜：

☐ 啤酒	1	2	3	4	5	
☐ 可樂	1	2	3	4	5	
☐ 冰紅茶	1	2	3	4	5	
☐ 湯	1	2	3	4	5	
☐ 炒飯	1	2	3	4	5	
☐ 炒麵	1	2	3	4	5	
☐ 餃子	10	20	30	40	50	

II. Character Exercises

A. Write the characters for the following words:

1. xǐhuān

2. háishì

3. píjiǔ

4. lǜchá

5. chǎomiàn

6. kělè

7. chǎofàn

8. xiǎng

9. fànguǎn

10. bīnghóngchá

11. xiānsheng

12. xiǎojiě

13. fúwùyuán

14. jiǎozi

15. shuāng

16. pán

B. Write out the radicals for the following characters, count their stroke numbers, and look up their meanings in the dictionary and enter on chart:

Characters	Radical	No. of strokes	Definition
館	食	16	house
務			
坐			
員			
喝			
茶			
杯			
紅			
冰			
樂			
瓶			
酒			
盤			
麵			
筷			

III. Grammar Exercises

A. Ask an alternative question based on the choices given and then answer it:

1. 吃中國菜，吃法國菜

   _____?

   _____

2. 去打球，去圖書館

   _____?

   _____

3. 兩點下課，三點下課

   _____?

   _____

4. 是工程師，是老師

   _____?

   _____

5. 有四門課，有五門課

   _____?

   _____

B. Fill in the blanks with the proper measure words (some of them may be used more than once):

位　隻　個　杯　瓶　輛　盤　碗　雙　本

1. 常先生是一 ___ 很好的老師。

2. 我點兩 ___ 炒飯和兩 ___ 可樂。

3. 爸爸有一 ___ 狗。

4. 我們家有四 ___ 人。

5. 她想喝一 ___ 茶。

6. 我的朋友要一 ___ 啤酒。

7. 那個美國人有一 ___ 車。

8. 那三 ___ 法國人想喝一 ___ 冰紅茶和兩 ___ 咖啡。

9. 這五 ___ 學生有三 ___ 工程書。

10. 給我們三 ___ 湯和一 ___ 筷子。

C. Translate the following sentences into Chinese:

1. Do you like drinking tea or coffee?

   _____

2. Which subject do you like to study, literature or engineering?

   _____

3. After eating the fried rice, I want to drink a cup of tea.

   _____

4. I often go to Chinese restaurants.

   _____

IV. Comprehensive Exercises

Three old friends of yours are coming to your apartment for a visit in the evening. But you are unfortunately unable to prepare food for them. You leave a note to your roommate and ask him/her to do you a favor by ordering food from the Chinese restaurant (at least 70 characters). Please include the following words and phrases in the note:

點　要　想　喜歡　杯　瓶　盤　碗　雙　謝謝

_____

_____

_____

_____

_____

_____

_____

嗎 (1)	嗎 (2)	吗 (3)	ma: (Part.) 你是學生嗎？ (4)	kǒu 口 (6) mouth		嗎 嗎 (7)		(8)		
	口 (5)	口¯	吖	吁	咡	咡	嗎	嗎	嗎	嗎	嗎

Guide for Students

1) Character with its stroke order indicated by numbers

2) Traditional form of the character

3) Simplified form of the character

4) Pinyin pronunciation, grammatical usage, and example sentence or phrase

5) Stroke order illustrated by writing the character progressively

6) Radical of the character with its Pinyin pronunciation and meaning

7) Ghosted images for students to trace over

8) Dotted graph lines to aid students' practice

Lesson 1　Hello!

			nǐ: you 你好！	rén　人（亻） person			
你	你	你		你　你			
ノ	イ	伫	伫	你	你		

			hǎo: good 你好！	nǚ　女 female			
好	好	好		好　好			
く	乆	女	女	奵	好		

			shì: to be 我是學生。	rì　日 sun			
是	是	是		是　是			
丨	冂	曰	日	旦	早	早	昰	是

			xué （學生: student） 學生	zǐ　子 child			
學	學	学		學　學			
メ	爻	陔	陔	臼	臼	臼	臼	臼	與	學	學

			shēng: （學生: student） 學生	shēng　生 produce			
生	生	生		生　生			
ノ	上	午	生	生			

| 嗎 | 嗎 吗 | ma: (Part.)
你是學生嗎？ | kǒu 口
mouth | 嗎 嗎 | | | | |
| 口 口一 吖 吓 咔 咔 嗎 嗎 嗎 嗎 嗎 | | | | | | | | |

| 我 | 我 我 | wǒ: I, me
我是學生。 | gē 戈
spear | 我 我 | | | |
| ノ 二 于 手 扰 我 我 | | | | | | | |

| 呢 | 呢 呢 | ne: (Part.)
你呢？ | kǒu 口
mouth | 呢 呢 | | | |
| 口 口つ 口コ 叩 叻 呢 | | | | | | | |

| 也 | 也 也 | yě: also, too
我也是學生。 | yǐ 乙
second | 也 也 | | | |
| フ 也 也 | | | | | | | |

| 他 | 他 他 | tā: he, him
他是學生。 | rén 人 (亻)
person | 他 他 | | | |
| 亻 他 | | | | | | | |

| 不 | 不 不 | bù: no, not
不是 | yī 一
one | 不 不 | | | |
| 一 フ 不 不 | | | | | | | |

				lǎo: (老師: teacher) 老師	lǎo ⺹ old			
老	老	老				老 老		
	一	十	土	耂	耂	老		

			shī: (老師: teacher) 老師	jīn 巾 napkin				
師	師	师			師 師			
	′	⺊	⼧	⼧	𠂤	𠂤	𠂤	𠂤	師

第一課 ▪ 你好!

Lesson 2   What's Your Surname?

您	您 您		nín: (for politeness) you 您好	xīn 心 (忄) heart	您 您
	亻 你 你 您 您 您				

貴	貴 贵		guì: noble, honored; expensive 您貴姓？	bèi 貝 shell	貴 貴
	丶 冖 口 中 虫 虫 耂 耂 青 昔 貴 貴				

姓	姓 姓		xìng: family name 我姓李。	nǚ 女 female	姓 姓
	乚 夂 女 女 奵 奵 姓 姓				

請	請 请		qǐng: please (請問: May I ask...) 請問	yán 言 word	請 請
	丶 二 言 言 言 言 詰 詰 請 請 請				

問	問 问		wèn: ask (請問: May I ask...) 請問	kǒu 口 mouth	問 問
	丨 冂 冂 冂 冂 門 門 門 門 問 問				

				de: (Part.) 我的名字	bái 白 white			
的	的	的				的 的		
	′	′	亻	亻	白	白	的 的	

				Yīng: English 英文	cǎo 艸 (艹) grass			
英	英	英				英 英		
	一	十	艹	艹	苎	苎	英 英	

				wén: language, writing 中文	wén 文 literature			
文	文	文				文 文		
	′	一	亠	文				

				míng: name 名字	kǒu 口 mouth			
名	名	名				名 名		
	′	ク	夕	夕	名	名		

				zì: character, word (名字 míngzi: name) 名字	zǐ 子 child			
字	字	字				字 字		
	′	′	宀	宁	宁	字		

				zhōng: (中文: Chinese; 中國: China) 中文 中國	kǎn 丨 down stroke			
中	中	中				中 中		
	′	丨	口	中				

叫	叫	叫	jiào: to call 我叫小美。	kǒu 口 mouth			
叫				叫 叫			
㇑ 口 口 叫 叫							

什	什	什	shén: (什麼: what) 什麼	rén 人 (亻) person			
什				什 什			
丿 亻 仁 什							

麼	麼	么	me: (什麼: what) 什麼	má 麻 hemp			
麼				麼 麼			
、 亠 广 广 庐 庐 府 麻 麻 麻 麼 麼							

她	她	她	tā: she, her 她呢？	nǚ 女 female			
她				她 她			
㇈ 乂 女 如 奵 她							

誰	誰	谁	shéi: who, whom 她是誰？	yán 言 word			
誰				誰 誰			
言 言 訁 訁 訁 訁 誰 誰 誰							

同	同	同	tóng: same, similar (同學: classmate) 同學	kǒu 口 mouth			
同				同 同			
㇐ 冂 冂 同 同 同							

Name: _____   Date: _____

Lesson 3   Which Country Are You From?

哪	哪 哪		nǎ: which 哪國人	kǒu 口 mouth			
				哪 哪			
	丨 丨口 丨口 叮 叮 叮 哪 哪						

國	國 国		guó: country 美國	wéi 口 enclosure			
				國 國			
	丨 冂 冂 同 国 或 國 國 國						

人	人 人		rén: person 中國人	rén 人 (亻) person			
				人 人			
	丿 人						

很	很 很		hěn: very 很好	chì 彳 step			
				很 很			
	丿 彳 彳 彳 彳 彳 很 很 很						

對	對 对		duì: correct 對了。	cùn 寸 inch			
				對 對			
	丨 刂 刂 业 业 业 业 业 半 對 對						

第三課 ▪ 你是哪國人？   **Lesson 3** ▪ *Which Country Are You From?*   **111**

了	了 了	le: (Part.) 對了。	jué ∫ hook				
	了 了		了 了				
了 了							

法	法 法	fǎ: France 法國	shuǐ 水(氵) water				
			法 法				
丶 丶 氵 氵 汁 汢 法 法							

美	美 美	měi: USA 美國	yáng 羊 sheep				
			美 美				
丶 丷 丷 半 羊 羊 美 美							

說	說 说	shuō: speak 說中文	yán 言 word				
			說 说				
言 言 訂 訂 詍 詍 詓 說							

會	會 会	huì: can 會說中文	rì 日 sun				
			會 會				
人 스 仒 仐 侖 侖 侖 侖 侖 侖 會 會 會							

一	一 一	yī: one 一點兒	yī 一 one				
			一 一				
一							

				hēi 黑 black			
點	點 点	diǎn: dot 一點兒	點 點				
ㅣ 冂 冃 冃 曰 里 黒 黒 點 點							

			ér: (retroflex ending) (一點兒: a little bit) 一點兒	ér 儿 walking man			
兒	兒 儿		兒 兒				
ノ ㇒ 冂 臼 臼 臼 臼 兒							

			hé: and 我和你	kǒu 口 mouth			
和	和 和		和 和				
ノ 二 千 禾 禾 和 和							

　第三課 ▪ 你是哪國人？　**Lesson 3** ▪ *Which Country Are You From?*

Lesson 4   What Do You Study?

那	那 那	**nà: that** 那是	yì 邑(阝) city 那 那	
	了 ㄱ ㄱ 月 那 那			

書	書 书	**shū: book** 英文書	yuē 日 say 書 書	
	一 フ 子 ㋿ 肀 聿 書 書 書			

這	這 这	**zhè: this** 這是	chuò 辵(辶) motion 這 這	
	言 言 這 這			

本	本 本	**běn: (M.W.)** 一本書	mù 木 wood 本 本	
	一 十 才 木 本			

工	工 工	**gōng: work** (工程: engineering) 工程	gōng 工 work 工 工	
	一 丁 工			

程	程	程	chéng: (工程: engineering) 工程	hé 禾 grain			
				程 程			
	丶	二	千	禾	禾	利	和	和	稈	稈	程

難	難	难	nán: difficult 不難	zhuī 隹 short-tailed birds			
				難 難			
	一	十	廿	廿	艹	芇	苫	莒	堇	茣	茣	難

太	太	太	tài: too 太難	dà 大 big			
				太 太			
	一	ナ	大	太							

可	可	可	kě: but (可是: but) 可是	kǒu 口 mouth			
				可 可			
	一	丁	口	口	可						

功	功	功	gōng: (功課: homework; assignment) 功課	dāo 刀 (刂) knife			
				功 功			
	一	丁	工	巧	功						

課	課	课	kè: class (功課: homework; assignment) 功課	yán 言 word			
				課 課			
	言	訂	訂	訶	訶	誤	評	課	課

多	多	多	duō: many, much 很多	xī 夕 night		
				多 多		
	ノ	ク	夕	夕	多	多

們	們	们	men: (used after a personal pronoun or a noun to show plural number); (他們: they) 我們	rén 人 (亻) person		
				們 們		
	ノ	イ	亻	们	伊	伊	伊	們	們	們

少	少	少	shǎo: few, little 不少	xiǎo 小 small		
				少 少		
	l	小	小	少		

Lesson 5　　This Is My Friend

朋	朋	朋	péng: friend (朋友 péngyou: friend) 朋友	ròu 肉 (月) meat	朋 朋
	ﾉ	刀	月	月	月 朋 朋 朋

友	友	友	yǒu: friend (朋友 péngyou: friend) 朋友	yòu 又 right hand	友 友
	一	ナ	方	友	

來	來	来	lái: come 我來介紹一下。	rén 人 (亻) person	來 來
	一	ﾁ	瓦	夾	夾 夾 來 來

介	介	介	jiè: (介紹: introduce) 介紹	rén 人 (亻) person	介 介
	ﾉ	人	介	介	

紹	紹	绍	shào: (介紹: introduce) 介紹	mì 糸 silk	紹 紹
	ㄥ	幺	幺	幺	糸 幻 紹 紹

				xià: down; get off (一下: a little) 一下	yī 一 one	下 下			
下	下	下							
	一	丁	下						

			shì: room 室友	mián 宀 roof	室 室			
室	室	室						
	`	` `	宀	宁	宏	宏	室	宰	室

			yǒu: have 我有	ròu 肉 (月) meat	有 有			
有	有	有						
	一	ナ	才	冇	冇	有			

			jǐ: how many 幾個	yāo 幺 small	幾 幾			
幾	幾	几						
	幺	丝	丝	丝	丝	幾	幾	幾	

			liǎng: two 兩個	rù 入 enter	兩 兩			
兩	兩	两						
	一	冂	冂	币	兩	兩	兩	兩	

			gè: (M.W.) 一個	rén 人 (亻) person	個 個			
個	個	个						
	丿	亻	亻	們	們	個	個	個	個

都	都 都	dōu: all; both	yì 邑 (阝) city			
		都是	都 都			
	一 十 土 耂 耂 者 者 者 者 都					

常	常 常	cháng: often	jīn 巾 napkin			
		常說中文	常 常			
	⺀ ⺀ ⺌ ⺌ ⺌ 岀 峃 常 常					

跟	跟 跟	gēn: with	zú 足 foot			
		跟他	跟 跟			
	丨 口 口 马 马 马 足 距 距 跖 距 跟					

第五課 ▪ 這是我朋友　**Lesson 5** ▪ *This Is My Friend*

Lesson 6 My Family

家	家	家	jiā: home (大家: all; everybody) 我的家	mián 宀 roof 家 家	
	` ` 宀 宀 宀 宁 宇 穷 家 家				
大	大	大	dà: big (大家: all; everybody) 大家	dà 大 big 大 大	
	一 ナ 大				
從	從	从	cóng: from 從中國來	chì 彳 step 從 從	
	` ノ 彳 彳 彳 彳 彳 彳 彳 從				
在	在	在	zài: at; in 在美國	tǔ 土 earth 在 在	
	一 ナ 才 才 在 在				
四	四	四	sì: four 四個	wéi 口 enclosure 四 四	
	丨 冂 冂 四 四				

爸	爸	爸	bà: dad 爸爸	fù 父 father			
	ノ ハ ゲ 父 欠 爷 爸 爸			爸 爸			

媽	媽	妈	mā: mom 媽媽	nǚ 女 female			
	女 媽			媽 媽			

姐	姐	姐	jiě: older sister 姐姐	nǚ 女 female			
	く 女 女 如 如 姐 姐 姐			姐 姐			

作	作	作	zuò: (工作: work) 工作	rén 人 (亻) person			
	ノ 亻 亻 亻 竹 作 作			作 作			

男	男	男	nán: male 男朋友	tián 田 land			
	丶 口 曰 用 田 毘 男			男 男			

沒	沒	没	méi: (沒有: don't have, doesn't have) 沒有	shuǐ 水 (氵) water			
	丶 冫 氵 氵 沪 汐 沒			沒 沒			

			liàng: (measure word for vehicles) 兩輛車	chē 車 vehicle			
輛	輛	輛		輛 輛			
	一 厂 冂 戸 百 亘 車 輛						

			chē: car 美國車	chē 車 vehicle			
車	車	车		車 車			
	一 厂 冂 戸 百 亘 車						

			zhī: (M.W.) 一隻狗	zhuī 隹 short-tailed birds			
隻	隻	只		隻 隻			
	亻 仁 忄 仁 仨 佳 隹 隻 隻						

			gǒu: dog 一隻狗	quǎn 犬 (犭) dog			
狗	狗	狗		狗 狗			
	丿 犭 犭 犭 狗 狗 狗 狗						

			ài: love 我愛我的家	xīn 心 (忄) heart			
愛	愛	爱		愛 愛			
	丿 爫 爫 爫 爫 悉 愛 愛 愛						

Lesson 7   Where Do You Live?

住	住 住	zhù: live 住在	rén 人(亻) person	住 住			
	ノ 亻 亻 伫 住 住 住						

宿	宿 宿	sù: put up for the night (宿舍: dorm) 宿舍	mián 宀 roof	宿 宿			
	、 ' 宀 宀 宀 宀 宀 宿 宿 宿						

舍	舍 舍	shè: house (宿舍: dorm) 宿舍	rén 人(亻) person	舍 舍			
	ノ 人 人 今 全 全 舍 舍						

號	號 号	hào: number 號碼	hǔ 虍 tiger's stripes	號 號			
	口 口 号 号 号 號 號 號 號 號						

房	房 房	fáng: house 房間	hù 戶 door	房 房			
	、 ' 宀 戶 戶 戶 房 房						

間 (1 2 3 5 6 4 7 8 9 11 10 12)	間 间	jiān: room 房間	mén 門 door 間 間					
	尸 門 門 門 閒 間							

電	電 电	diàn: electricity 電話	yǔ 雨 rain 電 電					
	一 厂 冖 币 币 币 币 雨 雨 雪 雪 電							

話 (1 8 2 3 10 4 11 12 5 6 7 13)	話 话	huà: word (電話: phone) 電話	yán 言 word 話 話					
	言 言 訐 訐 話							

小 (1 2 3)	小 小	xiǎo: small 很小	xiǎo 小 small 小 小					
	亅 小 小							

碼 (7 6 10 1 2 3 4 11 13 14 15 12)	碼 码	mǎ: (號碼: number) 號碼	shí 石 stone 碼 碼					
	一 丆 石 石 石 碼							

二 (1 2)	二 二	èr: two	èr 二 two 二 二					
	一 二							

				yī 一 one			
三	三	三	sān: three	三 三			
	一 二 三						

				èr 二 two			
五	五	五	wǔ: five	五 五			
	一 丁 万 五						

				bā 八 eight			
六	六	六	liù: six	六 六			
	丶 一 六 六						

				yī 一 one			
七	七	七	qī: seven	七 七			
	一 七						

				bā 八 eight			
八	八	八	bā: eight	八 八			
	丿 八						

				yǐ 乙 second			
九	九	九	jiǔ: nine	九 九			
	丿 九						

手	手 手	shǒu: hand 手機	shǒu 手(扌) hand 手 手			
	一 二 三 手					

機	機 机	jī: machine (手機: cell phone) 手機	mù 木 wood 機 機			
	一 十 才 木 機					

校	校 校	xiào: school 校外	mù 木 wood 校 校			
	一 十 才 木 朩 朾 朾 栌 栌 校					

外	外 外	wài: outside 校外	xī 夕 night 外 外			
	丿 夕 夕 列 外					

Lesson 8 Do You Know Him?

認	認 认	rèn: (認識 rènshí: know, recognize) 認識	yán 言 word 認 認				
	言 訂 訒 訒 訒 認 認 認						

識	識 识	shí: (認識 rènshí: know, recognize) 認識	yán 言 word 識 識				
	言 言 言 言 訂 訂 誰 識 識 識						

去	去 去	qù: go 去哪兒	sī ㄙ private; cocoon 去 去				
	一 十 土 去 去						

上	上 上	shàng: get on, go to (上課: attend class) 上課	yī 一 one 上 上				
	丨 卜 上						

以	以 以	yǐ: (以後: after; later) 以後	rén 人 (亻) person 以 以				
	𠄌 𠄌 以 以						

後	後 后	hòu: behind (以後: after; later) 以後	chì 彳 step			
(strokes 1 4 5 2 6 3 7 8 9)				後 後		
	彳 彳 彳 彿 後					

事	事 事	shì: matter, thing, business 事兒	jué 亅 hook			
(strokes 1 8 2 3 4 5 6 7)				事 事		
	一 一 一 一 一 三 三 事					

想	想 想	xiǎng: want 我想	xīn 心 (忄) heart			
(strokes 1–13)				想 想		
	一 十 才 木 札 相 相 相 相 想					

回	回 回	huí: return 回宿舍	wéi 囗 enclosure			
(strokes 1 2 3 4 5 6)				回 回		
	丨 冂 囗 回					

起	起 起	qǐ: (一起: together) 一起	zǒu 走 walk			
(strokes 1 2 8 10 9 3 4 5 6 7)				起 起		
	一 十 土 土 キ 丰 走 起 起 起					

吃	吃 吃	chī: eat 吃飯	kǒu 口 mouth			
(strokes 1 4 2 5 3 6)				吃 吃		
	丨 口 口 口 吃 吃					

飯	飯 饭	fàn: meal 吃飯	shí 食 (飠) food			
			飯 飯			
	ノ 𠆢 𠂉 𠆢 今 今 食 食 飠 飣 飯 飯					

菜	菜 菜	cài: dish 日本菜	cǎo 艸 (艹) grass			
			菜 菜			
	一 十 艹 艹 艼 苧 苧 芷 芝 芝 菜					

今	今 今	jīn: (今天: today) 今天	rén 人 (亻) person			
			今 今			
	ノ 𠆢 𠆢 今					

天	天 天	tiān: day 今天	yī 一 one			
			天 天			
	一 二 于 天					

次	次 次	cì: order, sequence (下次: next time) 下次	bīng 冫 ice			
			次 次			
	` 冫 冫 汐 汐 次					

怎	怎 怎	zěn: (怎麼樣: how) 怎麼樣	xīn 心 (忄) heart			
			怎 怎			
	ノ 𠂆 𠂉 乍 乍 怎 怎 怎					

樣	樣 样	yàng: appearance; sample (怎麼樣: how) 怎麼樣	mù 木 wood 樣 樣			
	木 术 杉 样 杆 样 样		样 样 樣 樣 樣			

行	行 行	xíng: okay	xíng 行 walk 行 行		
	ノ ゝ 彳 彳 行 行				

再	再 再	zài: again (再見: see you, goodbye) 再見	jiōng 冂 borders 再 再		
	一 厂 冂 冃 丙 再				

見	見 见	jiàn: see (再見: see you, goodbye) 再見	jiàn 見 see 見 見		
	目 貝 見				

Lesson 9　He Is Making a Phone Call

| 打 | 打 打 | dǎ: hit; play (打電話: make a phone call) 打電話 | shǒu 手(扌) hand | 打 打 | | | |
| 一 丁 扌 扌 打 | | | | | | | |

| 喂 | 喂 喂 | wèi (wéi): hello, hey | kǒu 口 mouth | 喂 喂 | | | |
| 口 口 叮 叼 吗 吗 吗 喂 喂 喂 | | | | | | | |

| 等 | 等 等 | děng: wait 等一下兒 | zhú 竹(⺮) bamboo | 等 等 | | | |
| ノ 一 一 午 竺 竺 竺 竺 笁 笁 等 等 | | | | | | | |

| 知 | 知 知 | zhī: know 知道 | shǐ 矢 arrow | 知 知 | | | |
| ノ 一 仁 午 矢 知 | | | | | | | |

| 道 | 道 道 | dào: road, talk (知道: know) 知道 | chuò 辵(辶) motion | 道 道 | | | |
| 、 丷 丷 丷 产 首 首 首 首 道 | | | | | | | |

謝	謝 谢	xiè: thanks 謝謝	yán 言 word	謝 謝		
	言 言 訁 討 訂 詷 誚 誚 謝 謝					

吧	吧 吧	ba: (Part.) 你是小美吧？	kǒu 口 mouth	吧 吧		
	口 口 吧 吧 吧					

忙	忙 忙	máng: busy 很忙	xīn 心 (忄) heart	忙 忙		
	丶 丨 忄 忄 忙 忙					

正	正 正	zhèng: in process of 正在	zhǐ 止 stop	正 正		
	一 丁 下 正 正					

看	看 看	kàn: see, watch 看電視	mù 目 eye	看 看		
	一 二 三 手 看					

視	視 視	shì: look at; watch (電視: TV) 電視	jiàn 見 see	視 視		
	丶 ㇇ 礻 礻 視					

| 做 | 做 做 | zuò: do 做什麼 | rén 人 (亻) person 做 做 |
| ノ 亻 亻 什 估 佔 佈 做 做 |

| 網 | 網 网 | wǎng: net 上網 | mì 糸 silk 網 網 |
| 糸 幺 糸 糸 網 網 網 網 |

| 就 | 就 就 | jiù: (我就是: this is he/she speaking) 我就是 | wāng 尢 crooked 就 就 |
| 丶 二 亠 古 亨 京 京 就 就 就 |

| 位 | 位 位 | wèi: (measure word for people, polite form) 哪位 | rén 人 (亻) person 位 位 |
| 亻 亻 伫 什 位 位 |

| 留 | 留 留 | liú: leave; remain (留言: leave message) 留言 | tián 田 land 留 留 |
| ノ 丘 丘 卯 卵 卯 留 留 留 |

| 言 | 言 言 | yán: speech, words 留言 | yán 言 word 言 言 |
| 丶 亠 言 言 言 |

				shí: time 時候	rì 日 sun		
時	時	时			時 時		
	一	丨	冂	日	日一 日十 日士 昨 時 時		

				hòu: time (時候 shíhou: time) 時候	rén 人 (亻) person		
候	候	候			候 候		
	亻	亻	亻	仴	仴 仴 仴 候 候		

				wǎn: night 晚上	rì 日 sun		
晚	晚	晚			晚 晚		
	日	日′	日″	日″	昖 昖 昳 晚		

				yào: want, desire 要不要	yà 西 (襾) cover		
要	要	要			要 要		
	一	丆	冂	襾	西 西 覀 要 要		

				gěi: give; for, to 給我	mì 糸 silk		
給	給	给			給 給		
	纟	纠	絈	給			

Lesson 10   I Get Up at 7:30 Every Day

活	活 活	huó: live (生活: life) 生活	shuǐ 水 (氵) water				
	氵 活			活 活			

期	期 期	qī: a period of time (學期: semester) 學期	ròu 肉 (月) meat				
	一 十 卄 卄 甘 其 其 其 期			期 期			

門	門 门	mén: (M.W.) 五門課	mén 門 door				
	尸 門			門 門			

每	每 每	měi: every, each 每天	mǔ 母 mother				
	ノ 一 仁 每 每 每 每			每 每			

床	床 床	chuáng: bed 起床	yǎn 广 shelter				
	丶 亠 广 广 庁 床 床			床 床			

				mù 目				
睡	睡	睡	shuì: (V.) sleep 睡覺	eye				
				睡 睡				
	目 旷 肝 眍 眍 睡 睡 睡							

				jiàn 見				
覺	覺	觉	jiào: (N.) sleep 睡覺	see				
				覺 覺				
	學 學 覺							

				shí 十				
半	半	半	bàn: half 十二點半	ten				
				半 半				
	丶 丷 兰 半 半							

				shǒu 手 (扌)				
才	才	才	cái: (used before a verb to indicate that sth. is rather late) 我十二點半才睡覺。	hand				
				才 才				
	一 丁 才							

				dāo 刀 (刂)				
刻	刻	刻	kè: a quarter (of an hour) 九點一刻	knife				
				刻 刻				
	丶 亠 亥 亥 亥 亥 刻 刻							

				dāo 刀 (刂)				
分	分	分	fēn: minute 十點二十分	knife				
				分 分				
	丿 八 分 分							

然	然	然	rán: (然後: then, afterwards) 然後	huǒ 火 (灬) fire		
				然	然	
	ノ	ク	タ	タ	㆐	夘	夘	夗	夘	然	然	然

圖	圖	图	tú: picture (圖書館: library) 圖書館	wéi 囗 enclosure		
				圖	圖	
	丨	冂	冏	冏	冏	冏	㗊	圖	圖	圖		

館	館	馆	guǎn: house, hall 圖書館	shí 食 (飠) food		
				館	館	
	食	飠	飣	飰	飵	飵	館	館				

午	午	午	wǔ: noon 下午	shí 十 ten		
				午	午	
	ノ	㇒	仁	午								

喜	喜	喜	xǐ: happy; like 喜歡	kǒu 口 mouth		
				喜	喜	
	一	十	士	吉	吉	吉	壴	喜				

歡	歡	欢	huān: joyfully (喜歡: like) 喜歡	qiàn 欠 owe		
				歡	歡	
	艹	茁	萑	藿	歡	歡	歡					

球	球 球	qiú: ball 打球	yù 玉 (王) jade 球 球			
	一　二　干　王　王一　玡　玡　玡　球　球　球					

寫	寫 写	xiě: write 寫信	mián 宀 roof 寫 寫			
	宀　宧　宧　寫　寫					

信	信 信	xìn: letter 寫信	rén 人 (亻) person 信 信			
	亻　信					

子	子 子	zǐ: (電子: electron) 電子	zǐ 子 child 子 子			
	了　了　子					

郵	郵 邮	yóu: mail 郵件	yì 邑 (阝) city 郵 郵			
	一　二　三　乒　乒　乒　垂　垂　郵					

件	件 件	jiàn: letter (郵件: mail) 郵件	rén 人 (亻) person 件 件			
	丿　亻　亻　仁　佐　件					

				dì: land 地址	tǔ 土 earth				
地	地	地			地 地				
	一	十	土	地					

				zhǐ: location 地址	tǔ 土 earth				
址	址	址			址 址				
	土	圵	圵	址 址					

				zhù: wish	shì 示 (礻) reveal				
祝	祝	祝			祝 祝				
	礻	祀	祀	祝					

				nián: year 二〇〇三年	gān 干 shield				
年	年	年			年 年				
	ノ	产	仁	午	乍	年			

				yuè: month 十一月	ròu 肉 (月) meat				
月	月	月			月 月				
	ノ	几	月	月					

				rì: day 二十日	rì 日 sun				
日	日	日			日 日				
	丨	冂	日	日					

Lesson 11 ◦ Do You Want Black Tea or Green Tea?

紅	紅	紅	hóng: red 紅茶	mì 系 silk			
	糸	糸一	紅	紅	紅 紅		

茶	茶	茶	chá: tea 喝茶	cǎo 艸 (艹) grass			
	艹	艾	苓	苓	芩 茶	茶 茶	

還	還	还	hái: (還是: or) 還是	chuò 辵 (辶) motion			
	丶	冂 冖 罒	罒	罒	罒 罒 罒 罒 還	還 還	

綠	綠	绿	lǜ: green 綠茶	mì 系 silk			
	糸	糸 糸	絼	絼 絼 絼	絼 綠	綠 綠	

服	服	服	fú: serve 服務員	ròu 肉 (月) meat			
	月	刖	朋	服 服	服 服		

務	務 务	wù: be engaged in 服務員	lì 力 strength 務 務		
	ㄱ ㄇ ㄡ 予 矛 矛 矛 矛 矛 矛 務 務				

員	員 员	yuán: person 服務員	kǒu 口 mouth 員 員		
	口 冒 員 員				

坐	坐 坐	zuò: sit 請坐	tǔ 土 earth 坐 坐		
	㇀ 人 人 从 坐 坐 坐				

先	先 先	xiān: (先生: sir, Mr.) 先生	ér 儿 walking man 先 先		
	㇀ 一 ㇏ 生 先 先				

喝	喝 喝	hē: drink 喝茶	kǒu 口 mouth 喝 喝		
	口 口 叮 叨 呷 呷 喝 喝 喝				

杯	杯 杯	bēi: cup 一杯紅茶	mù 木 wood 杯 杯		
	木 杯				

| | Name: _____ | | Date: _____ |

冰 冰 冰 — bīng: ice 冰紅茶 — bīng 冫 ice — 冰 冰
丶 冫 氵 氻 冰 冰

樂 樂 乐 — lè: happy (可樂: Coke) 可樂 — mù 木 wood — 樂 樂
丿 亻 白 白 白 帛 緇 緇 樂 樂 樂

瓶 瓶 瓶 — píng: bottle 一瓶 — wǎ 瓦 tile — 瓶 瓶
丶 丷 丷 兰 羊 并 并 瓶 瓶 瓶

啤 啤 啤 — pí: (啤酒: beer) 啤酒 — kǒu 口 mouth — 啤 啤
口 口 叩 叩 咱 咱 啤 啤 啤

酒 酒 酒 — jiǔ: liquor, wine, alcoholic drink 啤酒 — shuǐ 水 (氵) water — 酒 酒
氵 氵 汀 洏 沔 洒 酒 酒

麵 麵 面 — miàn: noodle 炒麵 — mài 麥 wheat — 麵 麵
十 才 求 來 麥 麥 麥 麥 麵 麵 麵

第十一課 ▪ 你要紅茶還是綠茶？ **Lesson 11** ▪ *Do You Want Black Tea or Green Tea?* **147**

| 餃 | 餃 饺 | jiǎo: dumpling 餃子 | shí 食 (飠) food | | 餃 餃 | | | |
| | 食 飠 飠 飠 飠 飣 餃 | | | | | | | |

| 盤 | 盤 盘 | pán: plate, dish 一盤 | mǐn 皿 vessel | | 盤 盤 | | | |
| | 丿 舟 舟 舟 舶 船 般 | | 般 般 盤 盤 盤 | | | | | |

| 炒 | 炒 炒 | chǎo: fry 炒飯 | huǒ 火 (灬) fire | | 炒 炒 | | | |
| | 丶 丷 少 火 灯 炒 炒 炒 | | | | | | | |

| 十 | 十 十 | shí: ten 十個餃子 | shí 十 ten | | 十 十 | | | |
| | 一 十 | | | | | | | |

| 碗 | 碗 碗 | wǎn: bowl 一碗飯 | shí 石 stone | | 碗 碗 | | | |
| | 一 丆 ア 石 石 砂 砂 砂 砂 砂 碗 | | | | | | | |

| 湯 | 湯 汤 | tāng: soup 一碗湯 | shuǐ 水 (氵) water | | 湯 湯 | | | |
| | 氵 氵 汨 沪 涅 湯 湯 | | | | | | | |

Name: _____ Date: _____

雙	雙	双	shuāng: (M.W.) 一雙筷子	zhuī 隹 short-tailed birds				
	隹	雔	雙	雙	雙	雙			

筷	筷	筷	kuài: chopsticks 筷子	zhú 竹 (⺮) bamboo				
	竹	竻	竻	筕	筷	筷	筷	筷	

Each entry lists traditional character, simplified character, Pinyin, English meaning, and lesson number.

1

一	yī	one	3

2

人	rén	person	3
了	le	Part.	3
二	èr	two	7
七	qī	seven	7
八	bā	eight	7
九	jiǔ	nine	7
十	shí	ten	11

3

也	yě	also	1
工	gōng	work	4
下	xià	down, get off	5
大	dà	big	6
小	xiǎo	small	7
三	sān	three	7
上	shàng	get on, go to	8
才	cái	not until	10
子	zǐ	son	10
久	jiǔ	long time	17
女	nǚ	female	20
已	yǐ	already	22

4

不	bù	no, not	1
文	wén	language	2
中	zhōng	middle	2
什	shén	什麼: what	2
太	tài	too	4
少	shǎo	few, little	4
友	yǒu	friend	5
介	jiè	介紹: introduce	5
五	wǔ	five	7
六	liù	six	7
手	shǒu	hand	7
以	yǐ	以後: after, later	8
今	jīn	today	8
天	tiān	day	8
分	fēn	minute	10
午	wǔ	noon	10
月	yuè	moon, month	10
日	rì	sun, day	10
比	bǐ	than	13
公	gōng	public	15
氏	shì	華氏: Fahrenheit	17
火	huǒ	fire	18
方	fāng	square	22
心	xīn	heart	22

5

生	shēng	man	1
他	tā	he	1
叫	jiào	call	2
本	běn	M.W.	4
可	kě	but	4
功	gōng	功課: homework	4
四	sì	four	6
外	wài	outside	7
去	qù	go	8
打	dǎ	strike, beat	9
正	zhèng	in the process of	9
半	bàn	half	10
用	yòng	use	12
白	bái	white	12
加	jiā	add	14

		hēi	black	13
黑	块	kuài	M.W.	13
塊	过	guò	pass, spend	14
過	为	wèi	for	14
為		bàng	good, excellent	14
棒	里	lǐ	inside	15
裡		yóu	swim	16
游	炼	liàn	refine	16
煉		zuì	most	17
最		duǎn	short	17
短	极	jí	extremely	17
極		jǐng	scenery	18
景		shū	loose, relax	19
舒	发	fā	feel, send out	19
發	复	fù	repeat	19
復	备	bèi	prepare	19
備	笔	bǐ	pen	19
筆	须	xū	must, have to	20
須		shǔ	heat, hot weather	21
暑		yú	feel happy	21
愉				
運	运	yùn	luck	21

		lù	road, street	18
路		gǎn	feel, sense	19
感		xiàng	be like	19
像	准	zhǔn	accurate	19
準		bān	move	20
搬	烟	yān	smoke	20
煙	脑	nǎo	brain	21
腦		yì	meaning	21
意	经	jīng	pass	22
經		xīn	new	22
新				

14

		me	什麼: what	2
麼	么	duì	correct	3
對	对	shuō	speak	3
說	说	rèn	recognize	8
認	认	tú	picture	10
圖	图	lǜ	green	11
綠	绿	jiǎo	dumpling	11
餃	饺	wǔ	dance	14
舞		màn	slow	16
慢		sòu	咳嗽: cough	19
嗽		lóu	floor	20
樓	楼	shí	solid, true	21
實	实			

13

		ma	Part.	1
嗎	吗	huì	can	3
會	会	gēn	with	5
跟		mā	mother	6
媽	妈	ài	love	6
愛	爱	hào	number	7
號	号	diàn	electricity	7
電	电	huà	word, speech	7
話	话	xiǎng	think	8
想		wǎng	net	9
網	网	shuì	sleep	10
睡		wǎn	bowl	11
碗		kuài	chopsticks	11
筷		gāi	should	12
該	该	jiào	compare	13
較	较	shì	try	13
試	试	suì	year of age	14
歲	岁	yuán	garden	15
園	园	yè	course of study	16
業	业	nuǎn	warm	17
暖		yuǎn	far	18
遠	远			

15

		qǐng	please	2
請	请	shuí	who	2
誰	谁	kè	class	4
課	课	liàng	M.W.	6
輛	辆	mǎ	code	7
碼	码	yàng	appearance	8
樣	样	xiě	write	10
寫	写	lè	happy	11
樂	乐	pán	plate, dish	11
盤	盘	liàn	practice	12
練	练	kù	pants	13
褲	裤	yǐng	shadow	13
影		chú	kitchen	15
廚	厨	rè	hot	17
熱	热	è	hungry	19
餓	饿	jù	opera, play	22
劇	剧			

16

學	学	xué	study, learn	1
機	机	jī	machine	7
館	馆	guǎn	house, hall	10
還	还	hái	還是: or	11
擋	挡	dǎng	gear	12
錯	错	cuò	wrong	13
錢	钱	qián	money	13
糕		gāo	cake	14
餐		cān	meal, food	15
澡		zǎo	bath	15
頭	头	tóu	head	19
燒	烧	shāo	burn	19
興	兴	xìng	pleasure	22

17

點	点	diǎn	dot	3
謝	谢	xiè	thank	9
應	应	yīng	should	12
幫	帮	bāng	help	13
鍛	锻	duàn	forge	16
賽	赛	sài	game, match	16
嚐	尝	cháng	taste	22
闆	板	bǎn	老闆: boss	22

18

雙	双	shuāng	M.W.	11
題	题	tí	problem, topic	12
邊	边	biān	side	15
離	离	lí	leave, away from	18
騎	骑	qí	ride	18
醫	医	yī	medical science	19
藥	药	yào	medicine	19

19

難	难	nán	difficult	4
識	识	shí	know, recognize	8
關	关	guān	關係: relation	20
麗	丽	lì	beautiful	22

20

覺	觉	jiào	sleep	10
麵	面	miàn	noodle	11
籃	篮	lán	basket	16
鐘	钟	zhōng	clock	18

21

歡	欢	huān	joyfully	10
襯	衬	chèn	襯衫: shirt	13

22

聽	听	tīng	to listen	18

23

體	体	tǐ	body	16
籠	笼	lóng	cage, steamer	22

24

讓	让	ràng	let	13
觀	观	guān	observe, look	15

25

廳	厅	tīng	hall	15

Each entry lists traditional character, simplified character, Pinyin, and English meaning.

Lesson 1

你		nǐ	you
好		hǎo	good
是		shì	is, are
學	学	xué	study
生		shēng	student
嗎	吗	ma	Part.
我		wǒ	I, me
呢		ne	Part.
也		yě	also, too
他		tā	he, him
不		bù	not
老		lǎo	old
師	师	shī	teacher

Lesson 2

您		nín	(polite) you
貴	贵	guì	noble, honored
姓		xìng	family name
請	请	qǐng	please
問	问	wèn	ask
的		de	Part.
英		yīng	英文: English
文		wén	language, writing
名		míng	name
字		zì	character, word
中		zhōng	middle
叫		jiào	call
什		shén	什麼: what
麼	么	me	什麼: what
她		tā	she, her
誰	谁	shéi	who, whom
同		tóng	same, similar

Lesson 3

哪		nǎ	which
國	国	guó	country
人		rén	person
很		hěn	very
對	对	duì	correct
了		le	Part.
法		fǎ	法國: France
美		měi	beautiful
說	说	shuō	speak
會	会	huì	be able to
一		yī	one
點	点	diǎn	dot
兒	儿	ér	(retroflex ending)
和		hé	and

Lesson 4

那		nà	that
書	书	shū	book
這	这	zhè	this
本		běn	M.W.
工		gōng	work
程		chéng	工程: engineering
難	难	nán	difficult
太		tài	too
可		kě	but
功		gōng	功課: homework
課	课	kè	class
多		duō	many, much
們	们	men	(suffix)
少		shǎo	few, little

Lesson 5

		péng	friend
朋		yǒu	friend
友	来	lái	come
來		jiè	介绍: introduce
介	绍	shào	介绍: introduce
紹		xià	down; get off
下		shì	room
室		yǒu	have
有	几	jǐ	how many
幾	两	liǎng	two
兩	个	gè	M.W.
個		dōu	all; both
都		cháng	often
常		gēn	with
跟			

Lesson 6

		jiā	home
家		dà	big
大	从	cóng	from
從		zài	at, in
在		sì	four
四		bà	dad
爸	妈	mā	mom
媽		jiě	older sister
姐		zuò	工作: work
作		nán	male
男	没	méi	don't have
沒	辆	liàng	M.W. for vehicles
輛	车	chē	car
車	只	zhī	M.W.
隻		gǒu	dog
狗	爱	ài	love
愛			

Lesson 7

		zhù	live
住		sù	stay overnight
宿		shè	house
舍	号	hào	number
號		fáng	house
房	间	jiān	room
間	电	diàn	electricity
電			

		huà	word
話	话	xiǎo	small
小	码	mǎ	number
碼		èr	two
二		sān	three
三		wǔ	five
五		liù	six
六		qī	seven
七		bā	eight
八		jiǔ	nine
九		shǒu	hand
手	机	jī	machine
機		xiào	school
校		wài	outside
外			

Lesson 8

	认	rèn	know, recognize
認	识	shí	know, recognize
識		qù	go
去		shàng	get on, attend
上		yǐ	以後: after, later
以	后	hòu	behind
後		shì	matter, thing
事		xiǎng	want, think
想		huí	return
回		qǐ	一起: together
起		chī	eat
吃	饭	fàn	rice, meal
飯		cài	dish
菜		jīn	today
今		tiān	day
天		cì	order, sequence
次		zěn	how
怎	样	yàng	appearance
樣		xíng	okay
行		zài	again
再	见	jiàn	see
見			

Lesson 9

		dǎ	hit, play, make
打		wèi/wéi	hello, hey
喂		děng	wait
等			

妹	飞	mèi	younger sister
飛		fēi	fly
玩		wán	play
到		dào	arrive
排	挡	pái	line
擋	开	dǎng	gear
開	应	kāi	drive
應	该	yīng	should
該	题	gāi	should
題		tí	problem, topic
白		bái	white
色		sè	color
停		tíng	stop, park
習	习	xí	practice
練	练	liàn	practice
能	进	néng	can, may
進		jìn	move forward
步		bù	step

Lesson 13

買	买	mǎi	buy
襯	衬	chèn	襯衫: shirt
衫		shān	shirt, clothes
店		diàn	shop
條	条	tiáo	M.W.
裙		qún	skirt
或		huò	or
者		zhě	或者: or
褲	裤	kù	pants
黃	黄	huáng	yellow
錯	错	cuò	wrong
比		bǐ	compare
較	较	jiào	compare
穿		chuān	wear
黑		hēi	black
試	试	shì	try
幫	帮	bāng	help
讓	让	ràng	let
錢	钱	qián	money
塊	块	kuài	dollar
張	张	zhāng	M.W.
影		yǐng	shadow, movie
票		piào	ticket

Lesson 14

歲	岁	suì	year (of age)
空		kòng	free time
星		xīng	star
過	过	guò	spend
為	为	wèi	for
舞		wǔ	dance
參	参	cān	join
加		jiā	add
定		dìng	surely
蛋		dàn	egg
糕		gāo	cake
送		sòng	give as a present
棒		bàng	good, excellent
客		kè	guest
氣	气	qì	air

Lesson 15

前	边	qián	front
邊		biān	side
迎		yíng	greet
觀	观	guān	observe
裡	里	lǐ	inside
廚	厨	chú	kitchen
公		gōng	public
旁		páng	side
走		zǒu	walk
廳	厅	tīng	hall
面		miàn	surface
餐		cān	meal, food
洗		xǐ	wash
澡		zǎo	bath
臥	卧	wò	lie
桌		zhuō	table
園	园	yuán	a piece of land
真		zhēn	really

Lesson 16

籃	篮	lán	basket
倆	俩	liǎ	two
教		jiào/jiāo	teach

游	yóu	swim
泳	yǒng	swim
非	fēi	wrong, not
快	kuài	fast
體 体	tǐ	body
育	yù	educate
池	chí	pool
健	jiàn	healthy
身	shēn	body
鍛 锻	duàn	forge
煉 炼	liàn	refine
現 现	xiàn	now
昨	zuó	yesterday
賽 赛	sài	game, match
業 业	yè	course of study
包	bāo	wrap
慢	màn	slow

Lesson 17

春	chūn	spring
久	jiǔ	long
放	fàng	put, release
假	jià	vacation
夏	xià	summer
秋	qiū	fall, autumn
冬	dōng	winter
其	qí	that, such
最	zuì	most
暖	nuǎn	warm
短	duǎn	short
熱 热	rè	hot
華 华	huá	華氏: Fahrenheit
氏	shì	華氏: Fahrenheit
百	bǎi	hundred
度	dù	degree
極 极	jí	extreme
刮	guā	blow
風 风	fēng	wind
雨	yǔ	rain
冷	lěng	cold
雪	xuě	snow

Lesson 18

火	huǒ	fire
旅	lǚ	travel
離 离	lí	leave, part from
遠 远	yuǎn	far
只	zhǐ	only
鐘 钟	zhōng	clock
騎 骑	qí	ride
自	zì	self
共	gòng	common
汽	qì	steam
路	lù	road
近	jìn	close
西	xī	west
部	bù	part
景	jǐng	view, scenery
船	chuán	boat, ship
南	nán	south
聽 听	tīng	listen
海	hǎi	sea
租	zū	rent

Lesson 19

感	gǎn	feel, sense
冒	mào	emit, give off
餓 饿	è	hungry
像	xiàng	be like; seem
舒	shū	loosen, relax
頭 头	tóu	head
疼	téng	ache, pain
發 发	fā	feel, send out
燒 烧	shāo	fever
咳	ké	cough
嗽	sòu	cough
病	bìng	sick
考	kǎo	give or take a test
復 复	fù	repeat
所	suǒ	所以: therefore
醫 医	yī	medical science
藥 药	yào	medicine
休	xiū	休息: rest

Traditional	Simplified	Pinyin	English
息		xī	rest
準	准	zhǔn	prepare
備	备	bèi	prepare
筆	笔	bǐ	pen
記	记	jì	notes

Lesson 20

Traditional	Simplified	Pinyin	English
把		bǎ	Prep.
帶	带	dài	bring
啊		a	Int.
搬		bān	move
出		chū	out
吸		xī	inhale
煙	烟	yān	smoke
關	关	guān	concern
係	系	xì	relate to
但		dàn	but
女		nǚ	female
必		bì	must
須	须	xū	must
第		dì	(prefix)
付		fù	pay
樓	楼	lóu	floor
馬	马	mǎ	horse

Lesson 21

Traditional	Simplified	Pinyin	English
暑		shǔ	heat, hot
畢	毕	bì	finish
決	决	jué	decide
申		shēn	express
研		yán	study
究		jiū	study
院		yuàn	institute
找		zhǎo	look for
司		sī	department

Traditional	Simplified	Pinyin	English
實	实	shí	solid
腦	脑	nǎo	brain
班		bān	class
意		yì	meaning
思		sī	think
愉		yú	happy
平		píng	calm, peaceful
安		ān	safe
運	运	yùn	luck

Lesson 22

Traditional	Simplified	Pinyin	English
因		yīn	because
已		yǐ	already
經	经	jīng	pass
麗	丽	lì	beautiful
城		chéng	city
市		shì	city
處	处	chù	place
新		xīn	new
些		xiē	some
方		fāng	side, direction
動	动	dòng	move
如		rú	be like
京		jīng	capital
劇	剧	jù	opera, drama
東	东	dōng	east
籠	笼	lóng	cage, steamer
嚐	尝	cháng	taste
始		shǐ	beginning
高		gāo	high
興	兴	xìng	pleasure
收		shōu	receive
心		xīn	heart
闆	板	bǎn	老闆: boss
保		bǎo	protect, maintain
重		zhòng	heavy

Each entry lists traditional character, simplified character, Pinyin, English meaning, and lesson number.

Traditional	Simplified	Pinyin	Meaning	
擋	挡	dǎng	排擋: gear	12
道		dào	知道: know	9
到		dào	arrive	12
的		de	Part.	2
得		děi	have to	12
等		děng	wait	9
地		dì	land	10
第		dì	(prefix)	20
點	点	diǎn	dot	3
電	电	diàn	electricity	7
店		diàn	shop	13
定		dìng	surely	14
冬		dōng	winter	17
東	东	dōng	east	22
動	动	dòng	move	22
都		dōu	all, both	5
度		dù	degree	17
短		duǎn	short	17
鍛	锻	duàn	forge	16
對	对	duì	correct	3
多		duō	many, much	4

E

Traditional	Simplified	Pinyin	Meaning	
餓	饿	è	hungry	19
兒	儿	ér	(retroflex ending)	3
二		èr	two	7

F

Traditional	Simplified	Pinyin	Meaning	
發	发	fā	feel, send out	19
法		fǎ	法國: France	3
飯	饭	fàn	meal	8
方		fāng	direction	22
房		fáng	house	7
放		fàng	put, release	17
飛	飞	fēi	fly	12
非		fēi	非常: extremely	16
分		fēn	minute	10
風	风	fēng	wind	17
服		fú	serve	11
復	复	fǔ	repeat	19
付		fù	pay	20

G

Traditional	Simplified	Pinyin	Meaning	
該	该	gāi	should	12
感		gǎn	feel, sense	19
糕		gāo	cake	14
高		gāo	high	22
個	个	gè	M.W.	5
給	给	gěi	give	9
跟		gēn	with	5
工		gōng	work	4
功		gōng	功課: assignment	4
公		gōng	public	15
共		gòng	common	18
狗		gǒu	dog	6
刮		guā	blow	17
觀	观	guān	observe	15
關		guān	關心: concern	20
館	馆	guǎn	house, hall	10
貴		guì	honor, expensive	2
國	国	guó	country	3
過	过	guò	spend	14

H

Traditional	Simplified	Pinyin	Meaning	
還	还	hái	還是: or	11
海		hǎi	sea	18
好		hǎo	good	1
號	号	hào	number	7
喝		hē	drink	11
和		hé	and	3
黑		hēi	black	13
很		hěn	very	3
紅	红	hóng	red	11
後	后	hòu	behind	8
候		hòu	時候: time	9
華	华	huá	華氏: Fahrenheit	17
話	话	huà	word	7
歡	欢	huān	joyful	10
黃		huáng	yellow	13
回		huí	return	8
會	会	huì	can	3
活		huó	live	10
火		huǒ	fire	18
或		huò	or	13

J

沒	没	méi	no	6
美		měi	美國: USA	3
每		měi	every	10
妹		mèi	younger sister	12
們	们	men	(suffix)	4
門	门	mén	M.W.	10
麵	面	miàn	noodle	11
面		miàn	surface	15
名		míng	name	2
明		míng	bright, tomorrow	12

N

哪		nǎ	which	3
那		nà	that	4
難	难	nán	difficult	4
男		nán	male	6
南		nán	south	18
腦	脑	nǎo	brain	21
呢		ne	Part.	1
能		néng	can, may	12
你		nǐ	you	1
年		nián	year	10
您		nín	(polite) you	2
暖		nuǎn	warm	17
女		nǚ	female	20

P

排		pái	排擋: gear	12
盤	盘	pán	dish	11
旁		páng	side	15
朋		péng	朋友: friend	5
啤		pí	啤酒: beer	11
票		piào	ticket	13
瓶		píng	bottle	11
平		píng	peace	21

Q

七		qī	seven	7
期		qī	a period of time	10
其		qí	其中: among	17
騎	骑	qí	ride	18
起		qǐ	一起: together	8

氣	气	qì	air	14
汽		qì	vapor	18
錢	钱	qián	money	13
前		qián	front	15
請	请	qǐng	please	2
秋		qiū	autumn	17
球		qiú	ball	10
去		qù	go	8
裙		qún	skirt	13

R

然		rán	然後: then	10
讓	让	ràng	let	13
熱	热	rè	hot	17
人		rén	person	3
認	认	rèn	認識: know	8
日		rì	day	10
如		rú	be like, as if	22

S

賽	赛	sài	game, match	16
三		sān	three	7
色		sè	color	12
衫		shān	shirt	13
上		shàng	on, go to	8
燒	烧	shāo	fever	19
少		shǎo	few, little	4
紹	绍	shào	介紹: introduce	5
舍		shè	house, shed	7
誰	谁	shéi	who	2
身		shēn	body	16
申		shēn	state, express	21
什		shén	什麼: what	2
生		shēng	學生: student	1
師	师	shī	老師: teacher	1
識	识	shí	know, recognize	8
時	时	shí	time	9
十		shí	ten	11
實	实	shí	實習: intern	21
始		shǐ	beginning	22
是		shì	to be, yes	1
室		shì	room	5
事		shì	matter, thing	8

Y

煙	烟	yān	smoke, cigarette	20
言		yán	speech, word	9
研		yán	study	21
樣	样	yàng	appearance	8
要		yào	want, will	9
藥	药	yào	medicine	19
也		yě	also	1
業	业	yè	course of study	16
一		yī	one	3
醫	医	yī	medical science	19
以		yǐ	以後: afterwards	8
已		yǐ	already	22
意		yì	meaning	21
因		yīn	because	22
英		yīng	英文: English	2
應	应	yīng	should	12
迎		yíng	greet	15
影		yǐng	shadow	13
泳		yǒng	swim	16
用		yòng	use	12
郵	邮	yóu	mail	10
游		yóu	swim	16
友		yǒu	friend	5
有		yǒu	have	5
愉		yú	happy	21
雨		yǔ	rain	17
育		yù	educate	16
員	员	yuán	person	11
園	园	yuán	garden	15
遠	远	yuǎn	far	18
院		yuàn	institute	21
月		yuè	month, moon	10
運	运	yùn	luck	21

Z

在		zài	at, in	6
再		zài	again	8
澡		zǎo	bath	15
怎		zěn	how	8
張	张	zhāng	M.W.	13
找		zhǎo	look for	21
者		zhě	或者: or	13
這	这	zhè	this	4
真		zhēn	really, truly	15
正		zhèng	in process of	9
隻	只	zhī	M.W.	6
知		zhī	know	9
址		zhǐ	location	10
只		zhǐ	only	18
中		zhōng	middle	2
鐘	钟	zhōng	clock	18
重		zhòng	heavy	22
住		zhù	live	7
祝		zhù	wish	10
準	准	zhǔn	準備: prepare	19
桌		zhuō	desk, table	15
子		zi	(suffix)	10
字		zì	character	2
自		zì	self	18
走		zǒu	walk	15
租		zū	rent	18
最		zuì	most	17
昨		zuó	past	16
作		zuò	工作: work	6
做		zuò	do	9
坐		zuò	sit	11

217

Name: _____ Date: _____

229

234

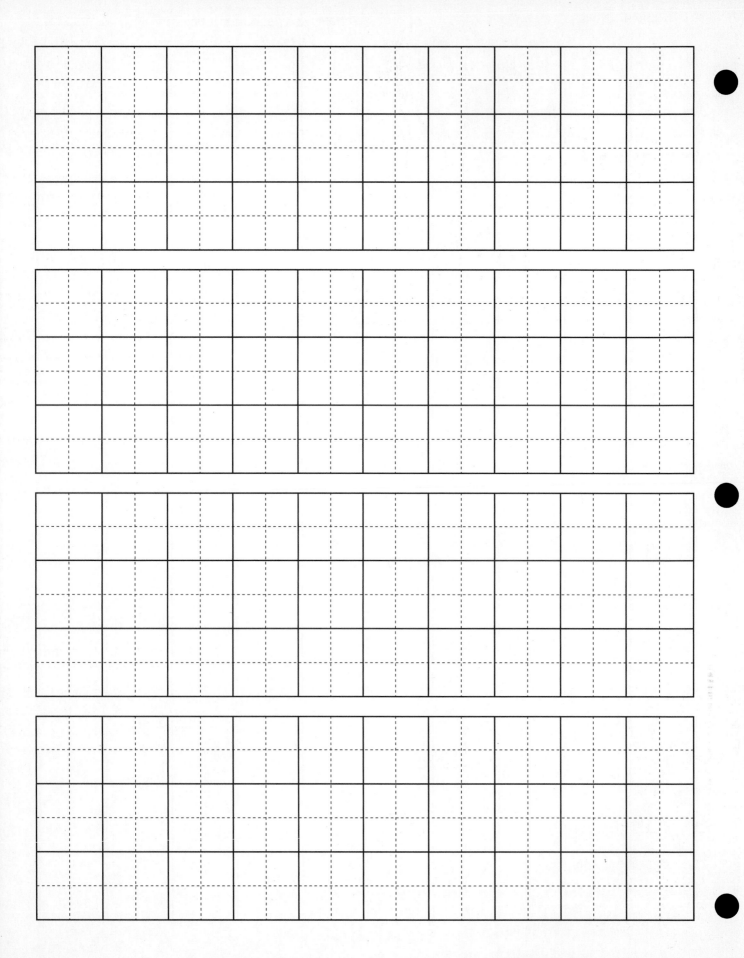